MW00931145

SLOW COOKER

RECIPES

10 Ingredients or Less
and Gluten-Free

HOPE
COMERFORD

From the popular blog *A Busy Mom's Slow Cooker Adventures*

Slow Cooker Recipes: 10 Ingredients or Less and Gluten-Free
Copyright © 2013 by Hope Comerford. All rights reserved.
First Print Edition: 2013

ISBN-13: 978-1489562319
ISBN-10: 1489562311

Photographer: Wyse Eyes Photography
Author Photos: Meghan Mace Photography
Cover and Formatting: Streetlight Graphics

Special Thanks:

THIS BOOK IS DEDICATED TO so many wonderful people in my life. To my husband Justin, daughter Ella, and son Gavin; thank you for being incredibly loving, patient and supportive as I've taken on this endeavor and for helping me fulfill my dreams. To the rest of my family and friends who have supported and encouraged me throughout this crazy dream of mine, I give tremendous love and thanks. To my dear friend Jocelyn; this book would not have happened without you telling me I could do this, so thank you so much for your support and encouragement. To my photographer Robert and his wife Kimberly; thank you for taking a chance on me and making my food come to life so beautifully on film. To my awesome friends and family who spent countless hours editing this book for me; I express my deepest and most sincere thanks! I couldn't have done it without any of you! To all of the loyal fans and followers of my blog, Facebook, Twitter, Pinterest and YouTube; thank you for your support and patience throughout this process!

Introduction

WELCOME, WELCOME, EVERYONE! I'M A BUSY mom, wife and full-time music teacher who makes no muss, no fuss recipes. Let's put it this way: I'd rather spend time playing with my kids than cooking dinner. Even if you're not a mom (or dad!), if you're busy, this cookbook is definitely for you! I make recipes with ingredients most anyone uses, and let my slow cooker do the rest while I'm away at work.

It all started three and a half years ago. My husband and I were both working on our Master's Degrees. We either ate out or cooked one of those frozen bag meals for dinner. It was becoming ridiculously expensive and unhealthy. If I did make a meal, I spent the entire evening cooking and cleaning up, which left me no time to play with my daughter before bed. I was at my wit's end. When searching for a recipe one day, I saw my slow cooker in the back of my cupboard. Only knowing how to cook a roast, I made one the very next day. When my husband and I came home with our daughter, dinner was ready! It was delicious. We looked at each other that night and said, "This. Was. Awesome!" Since then, the slow cooker has not left my counter.

I started my blog "A Busy Mom's Slow Cooker Adventures" in 2010 to share my recipes with my family and co-workers. I never imagined anyone else would want my recipes. Here I am, three years later and thousands of people turning to my recipes each week in order to get a home-cooked meal on the table. I'm thrilled you're reading this cookbook (My very first cookbook! That's right, I said FIRST....there will be more!) I hope you enjoy my recipes.....as well as my anecdotes.

Be sure to join me on my blog as well as all my social media sites:

www.slowcookeradventures.com
Facebook – www.fb.com/SlowCookerAdventures
Twitter - @BusyCrockPotMom
Pinterest – pinterest.com/BusyCrockPotMom
My YouTube Channel – www.youtube.com/slowcookeradventures

About this Book

THE FOCUS OF THIS BOOK is to bring you recipes you can make with 10 ingredients or less. I know it can be intimidating when you look at a recipe and there are tons of ingredients listed. I wanted you to feel you could make/conquer any of these recipes because they look doable. I also intended to bring you a book of recipes in which you can actually use each and every one of them. This is not the kind of cookbook with 200 recipes and only 2 of them which you make! I've even listed the ingredients I most commonly use, so you'll have them on hand any time you make a recipe from this book. I very much wanted this book to mimic my blog, so it is very conversational.

While making this cookbook, I started a gluten-free diet, so you will see recipes which are naturally gluten-free, or suggestions on how to make my recipes gluten-free. Don't worry, if you're not gluten-free, this cookbook is still for you! You won't even notice a difference in my recipes - I promise! In the beginning of the book, I've included a few recipes which will make adapting things a bit easier for my gluten-free friends.

I've tried to bring you recipes anyone can make. Some are super simple and some might be intimidating at first. Please remember, you can do it! I'm going to walk you through, step-by-step! Pretty soon, your family will start telling you you're a ROCK STAR in the kitchen! I've included pictures, in color, of all of the recipes in this book. No more wondering what yours should look like when it's done. I always cook and write directions to my recipes with a novice cook in mind (or for someone like my sister, who is not at all confident in the kitchen!) I hope this cookbook will put any of your cooking fears at ease! Again, you CAN do this!

Frequently Asked Questions

Which Slow Cookers do you own?

I currently own:

A 6.5 Quart Programmable Crock Pot Slow Cooker which I love! It automatically switches to warm when the pre-programmed cook time is up.

A 7 Quart Crock Pot Slow Cooker which is great for when I make soups and stews.

A 7 Quart Programmable Kenmore Slow Cooker which comes with a mini slow cooker to warm sauces and has a low, medium and high setting. Most slow cookers only offer low and high.

A 5 Quart Crock Pot Slow Cooker which is great for most everything.

A 3 Quart GE Slow Cooker (which is no longer sold.)

A Crock Pot Slow Cooker with two 2-Quart crocks in it (which is no longer sold.)

What kind of Slow Cooker do you recommend?

It really depends on how many people you're feeding and if you're gone for long periods of time. Here are my recommendations, but if you have questions, please feel free to contact me.

For 2-3 person household	3-5 Quart Slow Cooker
For 4-5 person household	5-6 Quart Slow Cooker
For a 6+ person household	7 Quart Slow Cooker

If you are gone for only 6-8 hours a day, a manual slow cooker would be just fine for you.

If you are gone for more than 8 hours during the day, I would recommend purchasing a programmable slow cooker that will switch to warm when the cook time you set is up. It will allow you to cook a wider variety of recipes.

Can I use frozen meat in the Slow Cooker?

There are many who say you shouldn't because the internal temperature of your meat does not reach the proper temperature in time. Personally, I use frozen meat every once in a while. I do not use large, thick frozen cuts of meat because of the fact I just listed. I've also read you can do so safely as long as you add a cup of boiling water and cook an additional 4-6 hours on LOW. So, proceed at your own risk and do some research on your own if you are unsure. Always check the internal temperature of your meat to be sure it's actually done.

How do I get stuck-on food off of my crock?

The soaking with dish soap method works very well for me. However, if you have an extraordinarily hard time getting your stuck-on food off, try Bar Keepers Friend (which can be found near the household cleaning items.) I've also heard filling your crock with hot water and letting it soak with a dryer sheet in it works as well.

Can I really leave my Slow Cooker on when I leave the house?

Yes. Slow cookers are meant to be left. If you're really super nervous about it and absolutely cannot bring yourself to do it, do all your slow cooking on the days when you're home and freeze it for use later.

Where can I find more of your recipes?

All of my recipes can be found at my website, www. slowcookeradventures.com, under the "Recipe Index" tab. They are all categorized there for you.

How can I contact you?

ABusyCrockPotMom@yahoo.com
www.slowcookeradventures.com
Facebook – www.fb.com/SlowCookerAdventures
Twitter - @BusyCrockPotMom
Pinterest – pinterest.com/BusyCrockPotMom
My YouTube Channel - www.youtube.com/slowcookeradventures
I'm always here to answer your questions,
so don't hesitate to contact me!

Slow Cooker Tips

- Disposable slow cooker liners are AWESOME! You line the crock of your slow cooker with them before placing all of your ingredients into your crock and when you're finished, you just throw the liner away! It makes clean-up a cinch. No, they are not made of plastic, rather a combination of nylon resins. They are also BPA Free and approved by the FDA for cooking.

- When you know you're going to have a busy morning, prepare your slow cooker meal the night before by placing all of your ingredients into the crock and then place the crock in the refrigerator overnight. In the morning, place the crock into your slow cooker, turn it on, and get out the door.

- Converting the cook time from low to high or vice versa is easy. Whatever the cook time is for LOW, you halve it for HIGH. Likewise, whatever the cook time is on HIGH, you double it for LOW.

- Save the recipes with a shorter cook time for weekends, or days when you know you're not going to be away from the house for too long. Save the recipes with longer cook times for the days you'll be away from the house longer.

- Ideally, you want your slow cooker to be about ¾ of the way full. So when choosing what size slow cooker you're going to use for a particular recipe, keep this in mind.

- Every time you lift the lid of your slow cooker, you have to add 20 minutes to your cooking time. So, don't peek!

- Use non-stick spray on your crock (or disposable slow cooker liner if you're using one of those) when you're making anything with cheese or sugar in it. It will help you get the food out easier and it will make clean-up a whole lot easier later.

- Boneless skinless chicken breasts cook quickly in the slow cooker and cannot be cooked for the same amount of time as bone-in chicken. So, if you're substituting boneless skinless chicken for bone-in chicken in a recipe, you'll need to adjust the cook time. Boneless skinless chicken dries out easily without lots of liquid or sauce.

Commonly Used Ingredients:

To make your life a bit easier, I thought I would go ahead and put together a list of ingredients I frequently use in this cookbook. I use these ingredients on my website as well. This is not a complete list of ingredients you will need for this cookbook.

Spices:
- Garlic Powder
- Onion Powder
- Salt
- Black Pepper
- Basil
- Oregano
- Parsley
- Thyme
- Minced Onion
- Chili Powder
- Cumin
- Italian Seasoning
- Cinnamon
- Nutmeg
- Dry Mustard
- Ginger
- Bay Leaves
- Poultry Seasoning
- Cayenne
- Red Pepper Flakes

Fresh Herbs:
- Thyme
- Rosemary
- Parsley

Produce:
- Onions
- Garlic
- Spinach
- Mushrooms
- Apples
- Carrots
- Celery
- Potatoes
- Cabbage
- Jalapeño Pepper

Meats:

- Boneless Skinless Chicken Breasts
- Bone-In Chicken
- Pork Shoulder Roast
- Pork Tenderloin
- Country Ribs
- Ground Beef
- English Roast
- Chuck Roast
- Ground Turkey
- Bacon

Pantry Items:

- Chicken Broth/Stock
- Beef Broth/Stock
- Black Beans
- Diced Tomatoes
- White Corn Tortillas
- Salsa
- Enchilada Sauce
- Powdered Milk
- Corn Starch
- Steel Cut Oats
- Brown Sugar
- Barbecue Sauce
- Olive Oil
- Lemon Juice
- Quinoa
- Tomato Paste
- Tomato Sauce
- Evaporated Milk

Refrigerated Items:

- Sour Cream
- Eggs
- Mozzarella Cheese
- Mexican Blend Shredded Cheese
- Butter
- Heavy Cream

Table of Contents

Pork:

Carnitas
Honey Mustard Pork Loin
Polish Sausage and Sauerkraut
Succulent Ribs
Super Easy Pulled Pork
Sweet and Saucy Pork Tenderloin

Soup:

Beer Chili
Black Bean Soup with Chicken and Salsa
Corned Beef and Cabbage Soup
French Onion Soup
Turkey Chili
Zuppa Toscana

Vegetarian:

Baked Mac n' Cheese
Black Bean Enchilada Bake
Cream of Mushroom Soup
Spicy Florentine Sauce
Vegetarian Lasagna

Basics

Basic Pasta Sauce

I LOVE HAVING JARS OF PASTA sauce around to use in recipes, or for nights where I don't feel like cooking. Now that I'm gluten-free, I can't always just grab a jar of sauce because many contain gluten. So, I've come up with a simple, yet flavorful basic pasta sauce for you.

Servings: This equals about 2 jars of store bought pasta sauce.

Ingredients:
- 1 can diced tomatoes
- 1 can diced tomatoes with basil, garlic and oregano
- 12 oz. can of tomato paste
- 1 cup water
- 1 large onion, chopped
- 1 Tbsp. garlic powder
- 1 Tbsp. onion powder
- 1 ½ tsp. Italian seasoning
- 1 tsp. salt
- 1/8 tsp. pepper

Directions: (Use a 3 Quart or larger Slow Cooker)
Place all of the above ingredients into your crock and cook on LOW for 7-8 hours, or on HIGH for 3.5-4 hours. You can freeze this in storage bags to use with other recipes, or use it the way it is. You can add 1 lb. of meat to it for a wonderful meat pasta sauce.

"Cream of" Soup

NOW THAT I'M GLUTEN-FREE, I can't eat any of the canned "Cream of" soups. It's not that I cook with them every day, but once in a while I do, and I needed to find a solution to this problem. Like anyone looking for inspiration, I turned to Pinterest. (Stop laughing!) I found lots of great recipes for "Cream of" Soup, but I had to find one that would work for me in a pinch. I've concocted my own version of "Cream of" Soup that you can keep in an airtight container and pull out what you need when you need it. If there is a particular "Cream of" Soup you use often, make a few batches of that particular kind and freeze them in individual serving sizes. Thaw them when you're ready to cook with them.

Servings: 1/3 cup of this mixture, together with 1 ¼ cup of liquid equals one can of "Cream of" Soup.

Ingredients:
- 4 cups dry milk powder
- 1 ½ cups corn starch
- 1 Tbsp. garlic powder
- 1 Tbsp. onion powder
- 1 Tbsp. minced onion
- 1 ½ tsp. salt
- ½ tsp. basil
- ½ tsp. dried parsley
- ¼ tsp. pepper

Directions:
Mix together all of the above ingredients. Store the mixture in an airtight container. Keep it in a dark place. It will stay good for at least a couple months. When you are ready to make "Cream of" Soup,

follow the instructions below.

Cream of Chicken: Bring 1 ¼ cup chicken broth to a boil. Stir in 1/3 cup of the "Cream of" Soup mix. Turn it down to medium heat until thickened.

Cream of Mushroom: Sautee ¼ cup diced mushrooms. Bring 1 ¼ cups of water or vegetable broth to a boil. Stir in 1/3 cup of the "Cream of" Soup mix. Turn it down to medium heat until thickened.

Cream of Celery: Sautee ¼ cup diced celery. Bring 1 ¼ cups of water or vegetable broth to a boil. Stir in 1/3 cup of the "Cream of" Soup mix. Turn it down to medium heat until thickened.

Cream of Tomato: Bring 1 ¼ cups of tomato juice to a boil. Stir in 1/3 cup of the "Cream of" Soup mix. Turn it down to medium heat until thickened.

Onion Soup Mix

I LOVE USING ONION SOUP MIX in my recipes because it's a very easy way to add flavor. No preservatives and no weird ingredients you've never heard of. Just a mix of spices you can feel good about serving to your family.

Servings: This makes approximately 4 packages of onion soup mix. Use ¼ cup of this seasoning mix to equal one packet of onion soup mix.

Ingredients:
- 2/3 cup dried, minced onion
- 2 Tbsp. parsley flakes
- 1 Tbsp. onion powder
- 1 Tbsp. turmeric
- 1 Tbsp. corn starch
- 1 tsp. celery salt
- 1 tsp. salt
- 1 tsp. sugar
- ½ tsp. pepper

Directions:
Mix all of the ingredients together and store them in an airtight container and in a dark place. Try to use within a couple of months.

Taco Seasoning

L AST YEAR, I ENDED UP with kidney stones, which was not fun! Ever since then, I've had to be careful with my salt intake. Because of that, I decided to make my own taco seasoning, since we tend to use it frequently in our house. Plus, I like saving money and being crafty. When you see how easy this is to make (and how good it tastes) you'll never use pre-packaged taco seasoning again! Ok, well maybe you might, but you'll think twice before you do.

Servings: The following recipe makes enough for 4 lbs. of meat. Use approximately 2 ½ Tbsp. per pound of meat. You can always cut it in half for less, or double it for more. Make it work for you and your family.

Ingredients:
- 4 Tbsp. chili powder
- 2 Tbsp. cumin
- 1 Tbsp. plus 1 tsp. garlic powder
- 1 Tbsp. plus 1 tsp. onion powder
- 2 tsp. salt
- 1 tsp. oregano
- 1 tsp. red pepper flakes

Directions:
Mix all of the ingredients together and store them in an airtight container and in a dark place. Try to use within a couple of months.

Breakfast Recipes

Apple Cinnamon Oatmeal

MAKING OATMEAL IN THE SLOW cooker is a cinch! You can put this in before you go to bed at night and wake up to a warm, healthy breakfast. If you're feeling wild and crazy, you could even switch out the apples for another fruit you enjoy. I did not add sugar to this recipe because I used sweetened almond milk and I felt it had just the right amount of sweetness. If you like your oatmeal sweeter, add some brown sugar to your bowl, that way you can control your own level of sweetness.

If you are gluten-free, be sure to buy steel cut oats that are gluten-free.

Servings: 4-6

Ingredients:

- 1 cup steel cut oats
- 4 cups vanilla almond milk (or whatever kind of milk you drink)
- 1 large or 2 small apples, diced
- ½ tsp. cinnamon

Directions: (Use a 2-3 Quart Slow Cooker)

Spray your crock with non-stick spray. Mix all ingredients in your slow cooker and cook on LOW for 7-9 hours, or on HIGH for 3 ½ -4 ½ hours. If you are having trouble getting yours to thicken, turn your slow cooker to HIGH, lift the lid for about a half hour and it should thicken up.

Crustless Spinach and Mozzarella Quiche

I ABSOLUTELY LOVE QUICHE. WHEN YOU taste this crustless quiche, you won't miss the crust at all. First, you'll be reminding yourself how much healthier of a choice you just made, and secondly, you'll be too busy eating to be thinking much more than "this is so good!" If you're cooking for a crowd, you're definitely going to want to double or quadruple this recipe. This got rave reviews from the teachers I work with when I brought it for pay day Friday.

Servings: 3-4

Ingredients:
- 8 eggs
- 1 cup milk
- 1 tsp. salt
- 1 tsp. garlic powder
- 1 tsp. onion powder
- ½ cup onion, chopped
- ¾ cup sliced mushrooms
- 1 small tomato, halved and sliced thin
- 1 cup fresh spinach
- 1 cup mozzarella cheese

Directions: (Use a 3-5 Quart Slow Cooker)

Spray your crock with non-stick spray.

First, mix together the eggs, milk, salt, garlic powder and onion powder. Pour that mixture into your crock.

Evenly sprinkle the chopped onions over the mixture. Place the mushrooms and tomatoes evenly all over the egg mixture. Place the spinach leaves on top of that. Push all the toppings under the egg mixture with the back of a spoon.

Top your quiche with the mozzarella sprinkled evenly all over.

Cook on LOW for 4-6 hours, or on HIGH for 2-3 hours. Your cook time will depend on how thick your egg mixture is in your crock.

Mexican Breakfast Casserole

T HIS RECIPE IS A GREAT alternative to a traditional breakfast. Using chorizo gives it an unexpected flavor that everyone will ask you about....in a good way, of course! If you've never used chorizo before, you're missing out. It's a Mexican sausage that's a little bit spicy and sweet. It's extremely tasty and great to use in dips as well. Again, waking up to breakfast already done is easy with this casserole. This doesn't just have to be for breakfast though. You could definitely serve this up as dinner.

If you are gluten-free, Boar's Head makes a chorizo that is sold at the deli. I called ahead to several stores to see if they carried it and found one fairly easily. It's not quite the same as using the fresh sausage, but it's still delicious. Also, make sure your white corn tortillas are gluten-free.

Servings: 6-10

Ingredients:
- 8 eggs
- 1 ½ cups milk
- 1 tsp. salt
- ½ tsp. pepper
- ¾ cup picante sauce (or just use regular salsa)
- 1 small onion, chopped
- 1 jalapeño, seeds removed, minced
- 8 oz. fresh chorizo, browned (see note above if you're gluten-free)
- 2 cups shredded Mexican blend cheese, divided
- 9-15 white corn tortillas (number will vary depending on the shape and size of your crock)

Directions: (Use a 3 Quart or larger Slow Cooker)

Mix together the eggs, milk, salt and pepper. Next, stir in the picante sauce, onions, jalapeño and 1 cup of the shredded Mexican cheese. Spray your slow cooker liner with non-stick spray.

Line the bottom of your crock with approximately 3 corn tortillas (or however many it takes to cover the bottom.) Pour half of the egg mixture over this and then crumble half of your chorizo on top. If you're using the gluten-free chorizo, arrange your slices to cover the top completely. Repeat this process with another layer of tortillas, egg mixture and the remaining chorizo. Top with a final layer of tortillas and the remaining 1 cup of Mexican cheese on top.

Cook on LOW for 7-8 hours, or on HIGH for 4-5 hours.

Peaches n' Cream Oatmeal

I GREW UP EATING PEACHES N' cream oatmeal and I still remember how nice and warm it made me feel in the morning from the inside out. This oatmeal was perfectly sweet and the peaches melted in my mouth. It's definitely not quite the same as the "packaged" kind, but it's probably ten times better for you!

If you are gluten-free, be sure to buy steel cut oats that are gluten-free.

Servings: 4-6

Ingredients:
- 1 cup steel cut oats
- 3 ½ cups vanilla almond milk (or whatever kind of milk you drink)
- 1 ½ cups frozen peaches, diced (If you use fresh, increase your milk by ½ a cup)
- 1 tsp. vanilla
- ½ tsp. cinnamon
- ½ cup brown sugar
- ¼ tsp. nutmeg

Directions: (Use a 2-3 Quart Slow Cooker)

Spray your crock with non-stick spray. Mix all ingredients in your slow cooker and cook on LOW for 7-9 hours, or on HIGH for 3 ½ - 4 ½ hours. If you are having trouble getting yours to thicken, turn your slow cooker to HIGH, lift the lid for about a half hour and it should thicken up.

Chicken Recipes

Barbecue Chicken

I LOVE BARBECUE CHICKEN, BUT LIVING in Michigan, I can't just get the grill out whenever I want. This is seriously the next best thing. The chicken stays nice and moist, and each bite is packed with barbecued goodness! You're going to love my homemade barbecue rub. It's what takes this from "good" barbecue chicken to "awesome!"

If you're gluten-free, be sure to use gluten-free barbecue sauce.

Servings: 4-6

Ingredients:
- 3-4 lb. bone-in chicken (I prefer thighs because they stay moist)
- ½ cup barbecue sauce

Barbecue Rub:
- 2 Tbsp. sugar
- 2 tsp. chili powder
- 1 tsp. paprika
- 1 tsp. garlic powder
- 1 tsp. salt
- 1/8 tsp. cayenne pepper

Directions: (Use a 5 Quart or larger Slow Cooker)

Preheat your oven to 400 degrees. Sprinkle both sides of the chicken with your rub and press in with your fingers. Cook the chicken in the oven about 10 minutes on each side to seal in your rub. (You can skip this step if you're in a pinch, but trust me, it's worth it!)

Place the chicken in the crock and pour the barbecue sauce over the top. Be generous.

Cook on LOW for 7-8 hours, or on HIGH for 3 ½-4 hours.

Buffalo Chicken Pasta

T HIS IS NOT ONLY ONE of my most favorite recipes, but it is one of the most popular recipes on my blog. It's creamy and spicy and packed with yumminess! To personalize this, you can use your favorite buffalo wing sauce. This also allows you to control the level of spiciness of your sauce. Here's a little secret about this recipe: this is actually better the second day than the first. And let me tell you, it's really good the first day, so that tells you how good it really is the second day. My nieces and nephew love this. My husband, who doesn't like spicy food, loves this. He sacrifices his dislike of spice for the awesome taste of this.

Here's a little tip for this recipe: If you start with frozen chicken and partially thaw it, it makes it really easy to slice it into strips.

If you are gluten-free, make sure you use gluten-free buffalo sauce and ranch dressing and to use gluten-free noodles instead. Because gluten-free noodles do not absorb as much as regular noodles, you may need to add more noodles to this.

Servings: 7-9

Ingredients:
- 3 large boneless skinless chicken breasts (approx. 2 lbs. or so,) cut into pieces
- 2 cans condensed cream of chicken soup (For gluten-free, make a double batch of the Cream of Chicken Soup on page 18)
- 3/4 cup buffalo wing sauce (You know, the orange kind. I used mild, but you could use hot.)
- 1 medium red onion, chopped finely
- ½ tsp. salt
- 1 tsp. garlic powder
- 2 cups sour cream
- 1/2 cup ranch dressing
- 1 cup mozzarella cheese
- 1 lb. penne pasta, cooked (For gluten-free, use gluten-free noodles)

Directions: (Use a 5 Quart or larger Slow Cooker)

In your crock, mix the cream of chicken soup, buffalo wing sauce and red onion. It will be beautiful with the bright sauce and the purple of the onions! Season your chicken with the salt and garlic. Add the chicken to the sauce in the slow cooker and make sure all pieces are covered well with sauce.

Cook on LOW for 7-8 hours, or HIGH for 3-4 hours.

About a half hour before serving, start the water for your pasta so you don't waste any time! While you're waiting for it to boil, turn your slow cooker to LOW (if it isn't already there) and add the sour cream, ranch dressing and mozzarella cheese. Stir until well-mixed.

When your noodles are cooked and drained, add them to the buffalo chicken mixture in your slow cooker. Mix well, let everything really meld together and serve!

Chicken Marsala

I ABSOLUTELY LOVE CHICKEN MARSALA! IT uses such simple ingredients, yet it's just packed with flavor. I made this for the first time for some company we had. Every one of us cleaned our plates. The boys went back for seconds! When the photographer finished photographing this dish, he immediately took a taste test. This is a super crowd pleaser. It's wonderful served as is, with some nice fresh sides, or you can serve it over pasta or rice.

I'll tell you, this is not something I would make on a busy weeknight, as it is a bit more labor intensive than my other recipes. With that being said, this is worth every bit of work you put into it! After you make this, you'll have one of those "I'm a ROCK STAR in the kitchen!" moments. Plus, I'm going to walk you through this step-by-step. YOU'VE GOT THIS!

If you are gluten-free, make sure you are using gluten-free corn starch.

Tip: If you're having trouble finding Marsala wine at your grocery store, look near the liquor by the cognac. Or, try near the cooking wines and dry sherry. You can also go to the local liquor store and try there.

Servings: 4-6

Ingredients:
- 4 lbs. boneless skinless chicken breasts
- ½ cup corn starch
- 1 tsp. salt
- 1 tsp. oregano
- ½ tsp. pepper
- 1 large onion, halved and sliced into half rings
- 12 oz. sliced baby bella mushrooms
- 2 ¼ cup sweet Marsala wine
- ½ cup olive oil (give or take)
- 1 ½ Tbsp. butter

Directions: (Use a 6 Quart or larger Slow Cooker)

The first thing you're going to do is take each chicken breast and thin it by cutting it in half. So, each chicken breast will become 2 thinner breasts. Once you've done this with each breast, you are going to pound it even thinner with a meat hammer/tenderizer. (If you don't have one, they're fairly cheap in the kitchen utensil aisle of the grocery store.)

Lay a piece of plastic wrap on top of your cutting board so you've covered the whole thing. Place one of your thinned breasts in the middle and cover it with another piece of plastic wrap of the same size. Pound the breast with your meat hammer until your breast is about ¼" thick, maybe a tiny bit more. (This is a great way to take out all of your aggression!)

In a dish (I used a casserole dish,) mix together the corn starch, salt, pepper and oregano.

Because each breast is on the large size when pounded out, I found I could fit 2 breasts into a frying pan at a time. Heat up about 2 Tbsp. of olive oil on medium high for each batch you cook.

Coat each side of your chicken breasts with the corn starch mixture and place in the frying pan with the hot oil until each side is just slightly browned (about 1-2 minutes on each side.) Place all your browned chicken into your crock.

In the same pan you just fried the chicken in, add about another Tbsp. of olive oil and sauté your onions until they are just slightly translucent. Add in 2 cups of Marsala wine and cook that on high for about 7 minutes, or until it thickens. Pour it over your chicken in the crock.

Cook this on LOW for 5 hours, or on HIGH for 2 ½ hours. 30 minutes before your cooking time is up, heat up 1 ½ Tbsp. of butter and 1 ½ Tbsp. of olive oil over medium high heat. Add the mushrooms. After about 5 minutes, add the remaining ¼ cup of Marsala and whisk in ½ cup of milk. Whisking it will keep it from curdling.

Pour this mixture over your chicken and continue cooking it for the last half hour. Serve and ENJOY!

Fragrant Lemon Rosemary Chicken

I'VE WATCHED A LOT OF cooking shows in my day and one of the best pieces of advice I've ever gotten about cooking is to use aromatics. My two very favorite aromatics are lemon and rosemary, so I put them together for this incredibly delicious and tender chicken. If you've never worked with a whole chicken before, don't be scared. I promise to walk you through the process. You'll no longer have to buy one of those rotisserie chickens at the grocery store anymore because this will replace it!

Might I suggest using any leftover chicken (if you don't completely obliterate it immediately!) to make some yummy chicken salad? Or, place it on top of some lettuce with a homemade lemon and olive oil dressing. Mmmmmm! Lots of possibilities here.

Servings: 4-6

Ingredients:
- 3-4 lb. whole roasting chicken (Or smaller. Whatever will fit in your slow cooker.)
- 1 lemon, cut into about 4 pieces
- 4-6 sprigs fresh rosemary
- 2-3 Tbsp. olive oil
- 2-3 Tbsp. poultry seasoning

Aluminum Foil
Butcher's twine (If you can't find it in the hardware section or utensil section of the nearest grocery store or department store, go ask the butcher. They'll point you in the right direction.)

Directions: (Use a 5 Quart or larger Slow Cooker)

Ball up 4 pieces of aluminum foil and place in the bottom of your crock. This is going to prop your chicken up and let the grease drain.

Grab your chicken and take out all of the giblets that are usually housed inside the cavity of the bird in a bag. Rinse your bird under the faucet and pat it completely dry with paper towels. That wasn't so bad, was it?! You can do this!

Stuff the inside of the bird with your lemon wedges and sprigs of rosemary. This is where you're going to truss your bird. Say what? Trussing means you're going to tie up your chicken. By trussing the chicken, it will keep the lemon and rosemary inside, and help keep the chicken together during the slow cooking process. If you absolutely can't do it, don't have the twine, or just don't feel like doing it, your chicken is still going to taste divine, so don't worry about it too much!

Trussing a chicken: Cut a piece of twine about 3-4 times the length of your chicken. With the chicken breast side up, tie a knot around the tail of the chicken (which looks like a "flap.") From there, make a loop around each drum stick (going over, under and around) and meet back up and tie a knot. Pass each end of the twine under each wing (keeping it tight) then around and over the top, tucking the wings tight against the bird, and flip it over. Tie the twine tight around the neck. You can cut off any extra twine. Phew, you did it. (The more you do this the easier and more natural it gets. If you're totally intimidated, do a search on the Internet for "how to truss a chicken" and watch a couple of tutorials.)

Rub the chicken down with olive oil and then sprinkle your poultry seasoning all over it. Place your bird on top of the foil in your crock.

Cook on LOW for 8-10 hours, or on HIGH for 5-6 hours.

Salsa Ranch Chicken with Black Beans

T his is probably the most popular recipe on my blog and the one recipe I've made most often! Because I'm always creating new recipes, I rarely repeat recipes. This is a real crowd pleaser and incredibly versatile. I've served it in tacos, over rice, on top of nachos, in a tortilla wrap, and as an appetizer with tortilla chips. Even the pickiest of eaters have tried this and loved it. I think you'll love it too!

If you're gluten-free, you will need to replace the can of cream of chicken soup with my recipe for Cream of Chicken Soup on page 18. Also, make sure you use a gluten-free taco seasoning, or use the recipe for my taco seasoning on page 20. Be sure your dry ranch dressing is also gluten-free.

Servings: 8-10

Ingredients:
- 2-3 lbs. boneless skinless chicken breast
- 1 packet low-sodium taco seasoning (or use 2 ½ Tbsp. of my taco seasoning recipe on page 20)
- 1 packet dry ranch dressing
- 1 cup (or more) salsa
- 1 can condensed cream of chicken soup (for gluten-free, use a batch of the Cream of Chicken Soup on page 18)
- 1 can black beans, drained and rinsed

Optional:
- sour cream
- shredded cheese

Directions: (Use a 5 Quart or larger Slow Cooker)

Place the chicken in the bottom of your crock. In a bowl, mix together the taco seasoning, dry ranch dressing, salsa, cream of chicken soup and black beans. Pour it over the chicken.

Cook on LOW for 5-6 hours, or on HIGH for 2 ½ -3 hours.

Top with the optional sour cream and shredded cheese and devour it any way you like!

Simple Coq au Vin

F IRST, THIS IS PRONOUNCED "COKE ahw vaen," with that last "n" being very nasal. It is a French dish which means "Rooster with Wine." With that being said, this is DELICIOUS! I absolutely love cooking with wine because it brings out the flavors in meat. I also like making things with fancy names because it makes me feel like I'm "fancy" even when I'm not! I think you'll find this recipe to be one your whole family will love, and you'll make time and time again.

Servings: 4-6

Ingredients:
- 6 chicken thighs
- 1/4 tsp. salt
- 1/8 tsp. pepper
- 2 Tbsp. olive oil
- 8 oz. mushrooms, sliced
- 1 large onion, cut into rings
- 3/4 cup red wine (I usually use Merlot or Paisano)
- 1/2 tsp. dried oregano
- 1/2 tsp. dried thyme
- 1/2 tsp. dried basil

Hot cooked rice to serve it on.

Directions: (Use a 5 Quart or larger Slow Cooker)

Sprinkle the chicken with the salt and pepper. Heat the olive oil in a large skillet over medium-high heat; brown chicken on all sides (this will keep the chicken skin from getting totally soggy.) Transfer the browned chicken to your crock.

Cook the mushrooms and onion in same skillet for about 5 minutes or until tender. Add the wine, stir and scrape the bits from bottom of skillet. Pour the wine and mushroom mixture over the chicken. Sprinkle it with basil, thyme and oregano.

Cook on LOW for 8-10 hours, or on High for 4-5 hours.

Stir-Fried Chicken and Vegetables

T HIS RECIPE CAME TO BE when I had to go gluten-free in the middle of making this cookbook. I originally had planned to make fajitas, but since I can no longer have the actual "wrap" of the fajita, I thought it a bit pointless. While at the grocery store, I stumbled across boneless skinless chicken thighs, which stay very moist in the slow cooker. When I eat stir-fry, I like lots of juice to go over my rice, so I knew this would be the best meat for this dish. Boy, was I right! The chicken melted in my mouth and the vegetables were cooked perfectly. I'm extremely excited for you to try this. It's an awesome "go-to" recipe, especially when you have random leftover vegetables lying around.

If you are gluten-free, be sure to use gluten-free soy sauce and chicken stock.

Servings: 1-6

Ingredients:

- 2 lbs. boneless skinless chicken thighs, cut into strips
- 1/4 tsp. salt
- 1 broccoli floret, cut into bite sized pieces
- 2 carrots, peeled and cut into matchsticks
- 1 ½ cups green beans
- 1 small onion, halved and sliced
- ½ cup soy sauce
- ¼ cup chicken stock
- 1 clove garlic, minced
- 1 tsp. ginger
- 1/8 tsp. pepper

Hot cooked rice to serve it over.

Directions: (Use a 2 Quart or larger Slow Cooker)

Place the chicken in the bottom of your crock. Place the onions on top of the chicken, then the green beans, carrots and broccoli. Mix together the soy sauce, chicken stock, garlic, ginger and pepper. Pour the sauce over all of the vegetables and chicken.

Cook on LOW for 5 hours, or on HIGH for 2 ½ hours.

Beef Recipes

Bacon, Spinach and Parmesan Stuffed Meatloaf

MEATLOAF IS ONE OF MY most favorite foods. I grew up eating it at least once a week. When I first began to cook, I had a recipe book I checked out from the library. In it, was a recipe for a delicious meatloaf, which I made over, and over again. In college, meatloaf was one of my "go-to" meals. Now that I'm older, I've found new ways to enjoy meatloaf. Stuffing it is one of my new favorite ways to enjoy it. You can really stuff your meatloaf with whatever you like, but now that I'm gluten-free, I'm really enjoying bacon and usually have it on hand. I also really enjoy fresh spinach and am always looking for an excuse to add it to my diet. And parmesan? Well, cheese is a must. In all seriousness, if one of these ingredients doesn't sound good to you, leave it out, or replace it with something that does. It's really all about making this work for your family. By using the quinoa, it keeps your meatloaf nice and moist, and it's incredibly good for you! Oh, and this is completely gluten-free!

Don't let the fact that you're going to stuff this meatloaf intimidate you. I promise it's really easy to do. And if it doesn't turn out perfectly, so be it. It's still going to taste good, whether or not it "looks" pretty! Take a risk. I think you'll find it pays off. Plus, I'm going to walk you through it.

Servings: 4-6

Ingredients:

- 2 lbs. ground beef
- ¾ cup cooked quinoa
- 1 Tbsp. minced onion
- 1 tsp. Italian seasoning
- 1 ½ tsp. garlic powder
- 1 ½ tsp. onion powder
- 1 egg
- 2 cups fresh spinach
- 1 cup shredded parmesan cheese
- 6 slices bacon

Wax paper
Non-stick spray

Directions: (Use a 4 Quart or larger Slow Cooker)

In a bowl, mix together the ground beef, quinoa, minced onion, Italian seasoning, garlic powder, onion powder and egg.

Place a piece of wax paper, about 2 feet long on your counter. Form your meatloaf into a ¼-½" thick rectangle on the wax paper. Leaving about an inch from each edge, layer on the bacon and spinach leaves, then sprinkle it with the parmesan cheese.

Now, you're going to roll up your meatloaf. Don't worry, I'm going to help you! Start by pulling up on one end of the wax paper and gently rolling the loaf toward you. You may need to press down on the loaf a bit along the way to keep the ingredients inside and to keep the loaf tight. When the loaf is all rolled, you're going to seal up both ends. Do the best you can with this.

Spray your crock with non-stick spray and place your stuffed meatloaf in.

Cook on LOW for 6-7 hours, or on HIGH for 3-3 ½ hours.

Balsamic Roast

T HIS RECIPE CAME TO BE when my old college roomie, John, came to visit me for a weekend. We went to a local oil and vinegar shop and tasted lots of different Balsamic Vinegars. We were in heaven! One of our favorites was the coffee balsamic vinegar. Sounds strange, right? I'm here to tell you, it's incredible! Since I wanted you all to be able to make this, even without buying an expensive coffee balsamic vinegar, I knew I had to figure something out. So, John and I stood at the counter, tasting and tasting and tasting, while I came up with the perfect coffee balsamic concoction. This made a delicious roast with wonderful balsamic flavor.

Servings: 6-8

Ingredients:

- 3-4 lb. English roast
- ½ cup balsamic vinegar
- 2 Tbsp. instant coffee
- 2 Tbsp. sugar
- ½ tsp. salt
- 1/8 tsp. pepper
- 1 medium onion, halved and sliced
- 5-6 carrots, cut into sticks
- 3-4 ribs celery
- 7-8 red potatoes

Directions: (Use a 5 Quart or larger Slow Cooker)

In the bottom of your crock, place the potatoes. Set your roast on top of that. Tuck all your other veggies nicely around the roast.

Mix together the balsamic vinegar, sugar and instant coffee. Pour this over your roast and veggies.

Cook on LOW for 8-10 hours, or on HIGH for 4-5 hours.

Cola Roast

T HIS IS HONESTLY AND TRULY one of those "throw it together and go" type of meals. When I first made this, I had the kids all ready to leave the house and realized I had nothing prepared in my crock for dinner. I threw this together in about 5 minutes. I'm not kidding. I've never peeled carrots so fast in my life! You'll be amazed at what a little can of cola can do for your roast.

Servings: 6-8

Ingredients:
- 3-4 lb. English roast
- 5-6 small potatoes, cut in half
- 4-5 carrots, peeled and cut into thirds
- 2-3 cloves of garlic, minced
- ½ tsp. salt
- 1/8 tsp. pepper
- 1 can cola (soda)

Directions: (Use a 5 Quart or larger Slow Cooker)

In the bottom of your crock, place the potatoes and carrots. Set your roast on top of that.

Sprinkle everything with the garlic, salt and pepper. Pour the can of cola over the top.

Cook on LOW for 8-10 hours, or on HIGH for 4-5 hours.

French Dip

T HIS IS ONE OF MY all-time favorite recipes. You see, as a kid, my dad would take me to Arby's and we would always get a French Dip. There's nothing like a good *au jus*! My mom never made it for us because no one else in our household had an interest in it. I was so proud when I had my dad over for dinner and could serve him my very own recipe for French Dip! Luckily, he loved it, and so has everyone else who has come to dinner at our house when I'm serving this. I think you'll find it will become a frequent dinner in your house.

If you're gluten-free, make sure to use gluten-free beer, Worcestershire sauce and beef stock. Serve it on gluten-free buns as well.

Servings: 6-10

Ingredients:
- 3-4 lb. chuck roast
- 1 can Progresso French onion soup (this is gluten-free)
- 1 cup beef stock
- 1 bottle of beer
- 1 onion, sliced into rings
- 8 dashes Worcestershire sauce
- 1 ½ tsp. garlic powder
- 1 ½ tsp. onion powder
- 1 ½ tsp. salt

Suggested Accompaniments
- buns or French rolls
- butter
- mozzarella cheese

Directions: (Use a 6 Quart or larger Slow Cooker)
Place your roast in the bottom of your slow cooker. Add in all of the remaining ingredients.

Cook on LOW for 7-9 hours, or on HIGH for 3 ½-4 hours.

When you're ready to serve, preheat your oven to 350 degrees. Butter both sides of your buns/rolls and sprinkle each side with mozzarella cheese. Cook these for about 10 minutes, or until the cheese has melted.

While your buns/rolls are toasting, take your roast out and shred it. Leave it separate from the au jus. When your buns are ready, top them with your shredded beef and enjoy them dipped in your au jus.

Italian Beef Sandwiches

IF YOU ASKED MY HUSBAND, he would tell you this is his favorite recipe. I find this kind of humorous actually because there's very little "genius" that went into this! Ha! Sometimes, simpler is better. I have to admit, this is one of my favorites too. This recipe only has 2 ingredients! You really can't beat that. When I was growing up, my sister and I used to pour the juice out of the pepperoncini jar into little bowls, and dip our leftover Turkey (after Thanksgiving or Christmas) into the juice. It sounds incredibly weird, but BOY, is it good! When my ultrasound tech suggested I combine a jar of pepperoncini with a beef roast, I had no doubt it would be amazing. And it is! My husband would like to suggest smothering this with either mozzarella or provolone cheese.

Servings: 6-8

Ingredients:
- 3 ½-4 ½ lb. English roast
- 16 oz. jar pepperoncini

Suggested Accompaniments:
- sub buns or gluten-free buns/rolls
- provolone or mozzarella cheese

Directions: (Use a 3-5 Quart Slow Cooker)

Place your English roast in the bottom of your slow cooker. Pour the juice of the jar of pepperoncini over the top.

Remove the pepperoncini from the jar and remove all the stems. Place them around your roast.

Cook on LOW for 8-10 hours, or on HIGH for 4-5 hours.

When it's done, shred the beef and pepperoncini with two forks. Serve them on toasted sub buns, or gluten-free buns/rolls with melted cheese. I prefer mine open face on a gluten-free roll without cheese. Very juicy and delicious!

Stuffed Cabbage

I GREW UP EATING MY MEME'S (Grandma's) Stuffed Cabbage. I helped her make it at least 3 times a year, but ate it far more often than that. When I was in college, I made a casserole version of these because I was afraid of doing it by myself. Now that I know how to do this, it's really not hard at all. Thanks to the commenters on my original blog post of this recipe, I now know of a VERY easy way to get the cabbage leaves off the head of cabbage....without burning my finger. I'm telling you right now, you CAN do this! I promise! I'm going to walk you through step-by-step. If you really get stuck, you can visit www.slowcookeradventures.com, search for "Meme's Stuffed Cabbage" in the "Search this Blog" box on the right hand side, and see step by step pictures on how to do this.

TIP: When you are thinking about making this, put your head of cabbage in the freezer 2 nights (or more) before. Take it back out of your freezer the night before you want to make it so it can thaw in time.

Servings: 6-8

Ingredients:
- 1 head of green cabbage

Stuffing:
- 1 lb. ground beef
- 1 cup brown rice, uncooked
- 1 large onion, chopped
- 2 large tomatoes, chopped
- ½ cup parsley, finely chopped
- ½ cup lemon juice
- ¼ cup olive oil
- 1 ½ tsp. salt
- 2 tsp. garlic powder

Directions: (Use a 3 Quart or larger Slow Cooker)

Hopefully you read my tip above and have already frozen your head of cabbage and thawed it. If not, you'll want to do this. Put it in your freezer a couple days before you want to make these. The night before, take it out to defrost. It's the easiest way to peel the leaves off the cabbage.

Brown the ground beef with the onions. Once it is cooked, combine all the remaining "stuffing" ingredients in a big bowl.

Next, peel off the outer layers of the head of cabbage that are dirty and discard them. Cut the stem off as best you can. Peel as many leaves off as you can.

Once you have all your leaves, you will want to thin the vein in each leaf. Turn the leaf with the "bumpy side" up on your cutting board. Next, starting at the thin part of the vein, run the tip of your knife very carefully toward the thickest part, thinning the vein so it makes the leaf more pliable.

Once all the leaves' veins are thinned, it's time to stuff them. Place the leaf so that it curves upward, like a cup. Place about 3-4 Tbsp. of stuffing into the leaf, depending on the size of the leaf. Use your judgment, as it may hold more or less.

Next, fold the horizontal (left and right) ends in first. Then, fold the top over toward the bottom. Lastly, fold the bottom up toward the top to complete your beautiful little cabbage package! You're going to layer all of these little "packages" into your slow cooker, packing them in as tightly as you can.

The very last thing you need to do is cover these with water. I poured in about 2 1/2 cups in my 3 quart slow cooker and it worked perfectly! You don't want your cabbage rolls «floating» so don›t overfill with water!

Cook on LOW for 6-8 hours, or on HIGH for 3-4 hours.

Pork Recipes

Carnitas

T HESE ARE SERIOUSLY SIMPLE, AND seriously delicious! My kids LOVE this recipe. We make lots so we can eat it for several nights and freeze some. It's not only great as traditional Carnitas, but it's also great on top of nachos, as well as in a tortilla. The meat is incredibly flavorful, tender and juicy! It's one of my all-time favorites.

If you're gluten-free, make sure your chicken broth is gluten-free.

Servings: 6-8

Ingredients:
- 3-5 lb. pork shoulder roast
- 2 cups chicken broth
- 2 bay leaves

Rub:
- 3 tsp. garlic powder
- 3 tsp. onion powder
- 3 tsp. cumin
- 2 tsp. salt
- 1 ½ tsp. chili powder
- 1 tsp. cinnamon

Suggested Garnishes:
- taco shells
- avocado slices
- limes
- shredded cheese
- fruit salsa

Directions: (Use a 5 Quart or larger Slow Cooker)

Mix all the rub ingredients together. Place your pork shoulder into your crock and rub it all over with the rub you just made, on all sides. Place the bay leaves around your pork shoulder and pour the chicken broth around it as well (but not on top so you don't wash the rub off.)

Cook on LOW for 8-10 hours, or on HIGH for 4-5 hours.

Remove the bay leaves and discard them. Shred the pork shoulder with two forks and place back into the juice. Serve in your taco shells with some fresh avocado slices on top and a squeeze of fresh lime juice. Top it with some shredded cheese and fruit salsa. Yum!

Honey Mustard Pork Loin

T HIS RECIPE CAME ABOUT WHEN I went to a restaurant and ordered honey mustard dressing on my salad (which I only do about once a year.) It was delicious! The next time I went to the store, I picked up some honey mustard dressing, and a pork loin hopped into my car too, somehow. When I got home, I decided the two needed to go together. And hence, this was born! This makes for a very simple and delicious dinner. Pair this with a nice salad and you've got a wonderful dinner.

If you're gluten-free, make sure to buy gluten-free honey mustard dressing.

Servings: 4-6

Ingredients:
- 2.5 lb. boneless pork loin
- 1 tsp. garlic powder
- ½ tsp. salt
- ¼ tsp. pepper
- ½ cup honey mustard dressing
- ¼ cup honey

Directions: (Use a 3-5 Quart Slow Cooker)

Place the pork loin into your slow cooker. Mix together the honey mustard dressing, honey, and all spices. Pour this over the pork loin. Cook on LOW for 7 hours, or on HIGH for 3 ½.

Polish Sausage and Sauerkraut

G ROWING UP, I NEVER HAD Polish sausage with sauerkraut. It wasn't until I was an adult and attended a few Polish events, I finally tried it. I had no idea the goodness I was missing! Many of my Facebook followers have been asking for a recipe like this, so I wanted to deliver. This turned out better than I ever imagined. The sweetness of the apples, matched with tanginess of the sauerkraut is insanely delicious! This would be a great dinner, or even an appetizer at a party, if cut into smaller chunks.

If you're gluten-free, make sure to use gluten-free beer and Polish sausage.

Servings: 4-6

Ingredients:

- 27 oz. Polish sausage, cut into 1 ½" angled pieces
- 4 slices of cooked bacon, chopped
- 2 golden delicious apples, peeled and cut into thin slices
- 2 lbs. sauerkraut, drained and rinsed well
- 1 cup red onion, halved and sliced
- 1 cup sweet onion, halved and sliced
- 1 bay leaf
- 2 cloves garlic, minced
- 2 Tbsp. brown sugar
- 12 oz. dark beer (If you're gluten-free, use a gluten-free beer you enjoy)

Directions: (Use a 6 Quart or larger Slow Cooker)

Place all of the ingredients into your slow cooker, pouring the beer in last.

Cook on LOW for 6-7 hours, or on HIGH for 3-3 ½ hours.

When you're ready to serve, remove the bay leaf and discard it.

Succulent Ribs

T HE BASIS OF THIS RECIPE comes from my friend and neighbor. We love to sit and chit chat, and in conversation, she mentioned how she makes her Grammy's ribs in the slow cooker. Next thing I knew, she was over here with a recipe card! I adapted it a bit, but it rings pretty true to her Grammy's recipe. My husband tasted these as they came out of the slow cooker and said they were amazing! My kids cleaned their plates. Need I say more? You can really use any type of ribs you would like, but country ribs are super cheap and always seem to be on sale. These ribs will melt in your mouth.

Servings: 4-6

Ingredients:
- 3 lbs. ribs (Any kind you like, but I suggest country ribs)

Sauce:
- 1 cup ketchup
- 2/3 cup brown sugar
- 1/3 cup lemon juice
- ½ cup dark molasses
- 1 ½ tsp. dry mustard
- 2 cloves garlic, minced
- 1/3 cup onion, minced

Directions: (Use a 5 Quart or larger Slow Cooker)
Place the ribs in the bottom of your slow cooker. Mix together all of the sauce ingredients and pour over your ribs.

Cook on LOW for 8-10 hours, or on HIGH for 4-5 hours.

Super Easy Pulled Pork

J UST AS THE NAME SUGGESTS, this is a super easy recipe! There are a total of 3 ingredients to this recipe....that's it! It doesn't get a whole lot simpler than that. Buy yourself some fancy buns, and call it a day. Everyone will rave at the dinner table about how good this is, and how amazing you are. Take your compliments! You don't have to tell them how easy it was.

If you are gluten-free, be sure your package of Onion Soup Mix is gluten-free, or see my recipe on page 19. Also, be sure to use a gluten-free barbecue sauce.

Servings: 6-8

Ingredients:
- 3 lb. pork roast
- 1 packet of dry onion soup mix (Or use ¼ cup of my recipe for Onion Soup Mix on page 19)
- 2 cups sweet barbecue sauce
- buns or gluten-free buns/rolls

Directions: (Use a 5 Quart or larger Slow Cooker)
Place the roast in your slow cooker and sprinkle it with the onion soup mix. Pour the barbecue sauce over the top.

Cook on LOW for 8-9 hours, or on HIGH for 4-4 ½ hours.

Shred the pork with two forks and re-stir through the barbecue sauce. Serve on buns/rolls and enjoy!

Sweet and Saucy Pork Tenderloin

M Y DAUGHTER MUST HAVE TOLD me ten times during dinner how good this was. That is not an exaggeration. She seriously loved this, and so did the rest of us! I'm personally a huge fan of sweet with my pork, especially fruit, and this is delectable. This is a crowd pleaser so I wouldn't plan on too many leftovers. So, may I suggest making a double batch?

If you're gluten-free, be sure to find a gluten-free apple pie filling and barbecue sauce.

Servings: 4-6

Ingredients:
- 4-5 lb. pork tenderloin
- 21 oz. can apple pie filling
- ½ cup sweet barbecue sauce
- ¼ tsp. salt
- 1/8 tsp. pepper
- 2 cups peaches, peeled and sliced (if you use frozen, thaw them)

Directions: (Use a 3- 5 Quart Slow Cooker)

Place the tenderloin in the bottom of your crock. Sprinkle it with the salt and pepper and pour the apple pie filling and barbecue sauce over the top.

Cook on LOW for 7-8 hours, or on HIGH for 3 ½ - 4 hours.

About a half hour before serving, add the peaches.

Soup

Beer Chili

B EER AND CHILI. Do I need to go on? This was absolutely delicious. You can really cater this chili to your own taste buds depending on what kind of beer you choose to use. This chili is a bit on the spicy side, so if you don't want as much spice, cut the chili powder and cumin in half. I made some delicious homemade sweet corn muffins to go with mine, but you could just serve yours with some crackers like my husband prefers.

If you're gluten-free, be sure to use gluten-free tomatoes with green chilies, beer and beef bouillon.

Servings: 4-6

Ingredients:
- ½ lb. ground beef, browned
- 1 (15.25 oz.) can black beans, drained and rinsed
- 1 (14.5 oz.) can diced tomatoes with green chilies
- 1 (4 oz.) can tomato sauce
- 1 (12 oz.) beer
- 1 large onion, chopped
- 1 beef bouillon cube
- 1 Tbsp. garlic powder
- 1 tsp. cumin
- 1 tsp. chili powder

Suggested Accompaniments:
- corn muffins or gluten-free corn muffins
- crackers or gluten-free crackers

Directions: (Use a 5 Quart or larger Slow Cooker)
Place all of the listed ingredients into the slow cooker and give it a quick stir.

Cook on LOW for 7-10 hours, or on HIGH for 3 ½-5 hours.

Black Bean Soup with Chicken and Salsa

T HIS SOUP IS VERY EASY to throw together and makes a very healthy dinner for your family. Before I really started cooking, I was terrified of beans....especially black beans. I absolutely love them now. I use them in a lot of my cooking. My children actually end up picking them out and eating them first in anything I make. I love when that happens! I hope your family begins to love them as much as mine.

If you're gluten-free, be sure to use gluten-free chicken broth.

Servings: 6-10

Ingredients:
- 4 cups chicken broth
- 1.5-2 lbs. boneless skinless chicken breasts
- 2 cans black beans, drained and rinsed (or 1 cup dry black beans, soaked overnight and rinsed)
- 2 cups salsa
- 1 cup frozen corn
- 1 cup mushrooms, sliced
- ½ red onion, chopped
- 1 jalapeño (whole)
- 1 ½ tsp. cumin
- 1/8 tsp. pepper

Suggested Accompaniments:
- shredded cheese
- fresh cilantro
- avocado
- sour cream

Directions: (Use a 5 Quart or larger Slow Cooker)
Place all of the listed ingredients into the slow cooker and give it a quick stir.

Cook on LOW for 6-7 hours, or on HIGH for 3-3 ½ hours.

Remove the chicken, shred it with two forks and place it back into the soup.

Serve garnished with any of the suggested accompaniments, or enjoy it as is.

Corned Beef and Cabbage Soup

I'M GOING TO DEDICATE THIS recipe to my new friend Mackenzie, whom I met almost a year ago and loves to cook as well. I commend her because she is young and single and loves to take risks in the kitchen. She told me about a recipe she found for corned beef and cabbage soup. I had never thought of that for some reason, but she mentioned how it called for leeks instead of onions, which intrigued me. Since I was in the middle of making this cookbook, I decided to make some and (if it turned out well) to put it in the book. Well, it turned out great, and now I get to share the recipe I created with you. You don't have to just eat corned beef on St. Patrick's Day. It's good all year round. I'll give you a little tip: Buy a few corned beef's around St. Patrick's Day when they're on sale and freeze them to use throughout the year.

If you're gluten-free, be sure to find a corned beef brisket that is gluten-free. My local grocery store's brand actually said "gluten-free" right on the package.

Servings: 10-12

Ingredients:
- 1.5-3 lb. corned beef brisket
- 4 cups beef stock
- 5 cups water
- 4 cups cabbage, chopped
- 6 small red potatoes, chopped into ½" pieces
- 3 stalks of celery, cut into bite sized pieces
- 3 carrots, cut into bite sized pieces
- 1 large leek, trimmed of the dark green leaves and sliced
- 1 Tbsp. garlic powder
- ¼ tsp. pepper

Directions: (Use 6.5 Quart or larger Slow Cooker)

First, let me walk you through cleaning a leek, because it's not a common ingredient to most people. You're going to want to trim off the dark green leaves and the "root" end. About ½" from the white end, use a knife and make a horizontal slit all the way toward the leafy end. Turn it and make another slit horizontally so that you have 4 "flappy" pieces, all held together by the white end. Take a bowl of clean water and swish them around in the water. Change the water until you don't see any more dirt.

Place the corned beef brisket into your slow cooker, topped with the remaining ingredients, then add the beef stock and water.

Cook on LOW for 8-10 hours, or on HIGH for 4-5 hours.

Remove the corned beef from your crock and shred it with two forks. Put it back into the crock and stir. Serve and Enjoy.

French Onion Soup

O NE OF MY FAVORITE THINGS to order at a restaurant is French onion soup. Well, now that I'm gluten-free, my days of ordering that at a restaurant are pretty much over. Thankfully, I have this delicious recipe to fall back on. I can't begin to tell you how amazing your house will smell as this cooks away all day! And when you add your favorite cheese on top…mmmmmm! It's seriously a delicious thing!

If you're gluten-free, be sure to use gluten-free beef stock and bread.

Servings: 6-8

Ingredients:
- 3-4 yellow onions, sliced thinly
- ½ tsp. pepper
- 2 sprigs fresh thyme
- 1 bay leaf
- 7 cups beef stock
- 1 cup dry white wine (such as a Chardonnay)
- Gruyere cheese (or Swiss cheese)
- French bread or gluten-free bread/roll

Directions: (Use a 5 Quart or larger Slow Cooker)

Place all of the onions into your slow cooker and sprinkle them with the pepper. Add the bay leaf and sprigs of thyme. Pour in the beef stock and wine.

Cook on LOW for 7-8 hours, or on HIGH for 3 ½ - 4 hours.

Remove the thyme and bay leaf.

Put your soup in an oven safe bowl and place a slice of bread on top, topped with enough cheese to cover the entire top. Place it in the oven with the broiler on for a few minutes, until the cheese starts to bubble. Enjoy!

Turkey Chili

I ABSOLUTELY LOVE A GOOD CHILI. I can eat it when it's warm or cold weather, it really makes no difference to me. Chili is definitely an easy meal to throw together, so we tend to eat it often. As I was putting this cookbook together, I noticed I didn't have a single turkey recipe in it, so that's how this came to be. If you're vegetarian, just leave the turkey out or use crumbles. If you would like to use ground beef, that would work too. It's all about making it work for your family.

If you're gluten-free, be sure the can of zesty chili style tomatoes you use is gluten-free.

Servings: 4- 6

Ingredients:
- 1 lb. ground turkey, browned
- 1 large onion, chopped
- 1 can kidney beans, drained and rinsed
- 14.5 oz. can diced tomatoes
- 14.5 oz. can zesty chili style tomatoes
- 4 oz. can tomato paste
- 1 tsp. salt
- 1 tsp. chili powder
- 1 tsp. garlic powder
- 1 cup beef broth

Directions: (Use a 3- 5 Quart Slow Cooker)

Place all of the ingredients into your slow cooker, beef broth last, and stir.

Cook on LOW for 6-8 hours, or on HIGH for 3-4 hours.

Zuppa Toscana

F OR YEARS, FANS HAVE BEEN asking for me to make a Zuppa Toscana recipe like Olive Garden's. The problem is, I've never actually eaten any at Olive Garden. And now that I'm gluten-free, I never will. The solution? I looked online at a million different copycat recipes and came up with my own that sounded good. It was delicious! I really enjoyed it and so did my son. He ate all of the sausage out of it first. And from a person who seriously doesn't like kale, I have to admit, I liked it in this recipe. This is another one of those dishes that will impress your family, or dinner guests.

If you're gluten-free, be sure to use a gluten-free Italian sausage.

Servings: 6-8

Ingredients:
- 1 lb. Italian sausage, browned
- 1 onion, chopped
- 2 Idaho potatoes, peeled and chopped into cubes
- 5 slices bacon, cooked and chopped
- 2 cloves garlic, minced
- ¼ tsp. red pepper flakes
- 3 cups chicken stock
- 3 cups water
- 1 cup heavy cream
- 4 cups kale, chopped

Directions: (Use a 3-5 Quart Slow Cooker)
In your crock, add the Italian sausage, onion, potatoes, bacon, garlic, red pepper flakes, chicken stock and water.

Cook on LOW for 7 hours, or on HIGH for 3 ½ hours.

When it is done, take about 2 cups of your liquid out and SLOWLY stir in the cream, whisking it constantly. You are tempering the liquid so that it doesn't curdle when you add it back into your soup. After you've done this, SLOWLY pour it back into your soup, whisking constantly again. Add the kale and let it cook for just a few minutes, until it's wilted.

Serve and enjoy!

Vegetarian Recipes

Baked Mac n' Cheese

I LOVE HOMEMADE MAC N' CHEESE! My kids love it too. And my husband who strongly dislikes mac n' cheese, says that mine is very good. It took me a while to perfect it in the slow cooker but I've got it down now. Even though I'm gluten-free, I refuse to give up pasta. There are so many wonderful alternatives. Now, I know my gluten-free friends have warned me that gluten-free pasta can be horrible, but I've only had good experiences with it thus far. Here's what I've learned; it doesn't absorb liquid as much as regular noodles. Therefore, I'm going to list this recipe two ways. One is a gluten-free version and the other is not.

Servings: 6-8

Non-GF Ingredients:
- ½ lb. radiatore noodles, cooked about 2-3 minutes shy of being done.
- 1 ½ cups milk
- 12 oz. evaporated milk
- 4 Tbsp. butter, softened
- ½ tsp. salt
- 1/8 tsp. pepper
- 1 cup queso blanco shredded cheese
- 1 cup Italian 5 cheese blend shredded cheese
- 1 cup sharp cheddar shredded cheese
- ¼ cup parmesan shredded cheese

Gluten-Free Ingredients:
- 1 lb. brown rice noodle shells, cooked about 1 minute shy of being done.
- 1 ½ cups milk
- 12 oz. evaporated milk
- 4 Tbsp. butter, softened
- ½ tsp. salt
- 1/8 tsp. pepper
- 1 cup queso blanco shredded cheese
- 1 cup Italian 5 cheese blend shredded cheese
- 1 cup sharp cheddar shredded cheese
- ¼ cup parmesan shredded cheese

Non-GF Directions: (Use a 2-3 Quart Slow Cooker)
Place all of your ingredients into the slow cooker and give it a stir. Cook on LOW for 5-6 hours, or on HIGH for 2 ½ - 3 hours.

Gluten-Free Directions: (Use a 2-3 Quart Slow Cooker)
Place all of your ingredients into the slow cooker and give it a stir. Cook on LOW for 5-6 hours, or on HIGH for 2 ½ - 3 hours. If it is still soupy, remove the lid and crank it up to HIGH for about a half hour.

Black Bean Enchilada Bake

THIS IS ANOTHER RECIPE MY family loves. Again, black beans are so delicious. They have a wonderful "meaty" quality about them that is so satisfying. Seeing as how I have a tiny obsession with Mexican food, I figured a nice "casserole" of enchiladas would be easier than rolling them. I was right! This only takes a few minutes to put together and uses inexpensive ingredients.

If you're gluten-free, be sure to use gluten-free white corn tortillas and enchilada sauce.

Servings: 6-8

Ingredients:
- 12-14 white corn tortillas
- 2 cans black beans, drained and rinsed
- 1 ½ cups salsa
- 20 oz. of enchilada sauce (you choose mild, medium or hot)
- 1 medium onion, chopped
- 14 oz. can of diced tomatoes with green chilies, drained
- ½ yellow pepper, chopped
- 2 cups Mexican shredded cheese

Directions: (Use a 5 Quart or larger Slow Cooker)

Spray your slow cooker with non-stick spray. Make a layer of tortillas that cover the bottom of your crock. The number of tortillas you use will depend on the shape and size of your slow cooker. It's okay for them to overlap.

Spread 1/3 of the black beans, 1/3 of the salsa, 1/3 of the onion, 1/3 of the diced tomatoes with green chilies, 1/3 of the yellow pepper and only ¼ of the Shredded Cheese and ¼ of the enchilada sauce over the tortillas.

Repeat this process two more times.

Add a final layer of tortillas, topped with the remaining enchilada sauce and shredded cheese.

Cook on LOW for 4-6 hours, or on HIGH for 2-3 hours. You want the cheese to be almost crispy on top, so if you find you have too much moisture, stick a towel under the lid for about 30 minutes with the heat cranked up to HIGH to help absorb some of the condensation.

Cream of Mushroom Soup

ONE OF THE THINGS I'M constantly asked for is more vegetarian recipes. While I myself enjoy meat, I also enjoy a good vegetarian meal. This cream of mushroom soup tasted better than any canned soup I've ever tried, or any cream of mushroom soup I've ever eaten at a restaurant. Best of all, it was so easy to make!

This recipe is naturally gluten-free.

Servings: 4-6

Ingredients:
- 8 oz. mushrooms (I recommend a variety, such as Bella, Oyster and Shiitake Mushrooms)
- ½ cup onion, chopped
- 1 Tbsp. fresh thyme, minced (or ½ tsp. dry ground thyme)
- 1 ½ tsp. salt
- 1/8 tsp. pepper
- 4 ½ cups vegetable broth
- 1 cup heavy cream
- ¼ cup corn starch

Directions: (Use a 3-5 Quart Slow Cooker)

Place the mushrooms, onions, thyme, salt, pepper and vegetable broth into your crock and stir.

Cook on LOW for 5-6 hours, or on HIGH for 2 ½ - 3 hours.

Remove about 2 cups of the soup broth and SLOWLY whisk in the heavy cream. This is "tempering" the milk so that your soup doesn't curdle. Slowly whisk your tempered milk/soup mixture back into your soup.

Turn your slow cooker up to HIGH. Now, slowly whisk in the corn starch, little by little. Keep whisking until it is well mixed. Let your soup cook about 15 minutes longer, whisking every few minutes. When the soup is thick enough to your liking, serve and enjoy!

Spicy Florentine Sauce

I'VE MADE A LOT OF pasta sauces in my career as a food blogger, but this one? It's special. There is something incredibly delicious about it...well, several things incredibly delicious about it. I still remember the day I made this. We had found some 3 cheese tortellini at Costco and we needed a sauce to go over it. You know I only use jarred sauces if there is an emergency, so I whipped one together. My husband was completely amazed at my improvisational skills. I've made this several times since that day and each time, I savor each bite. You can serve this on any kind of pasta you wish.

If you're gluten-free, do not use the condensed cream of tomato soup. Be sure to use my recipe for Cream of Tomato Soup on page 18.

Servings: 6-8

Ingredients:
- 1 (29 oz.) can of crushed tomatoes
- 1 (10 oz.) can diced tomatoes
- 1 (10.75 oz.) can condensed tomato soup (Or use my recipe for Cream of Tomato Soup on page 18)
- 10 oz. pkg. frozen spinach, thawed
- 10 fresh basil leaves, diced
- ¼ cup fresh cilantro, chopped
- 2 Tbsp. lime juice
- 1 small shallot, minced
- 3 cloves garlic, minced
- 1/2 tsp. salt

Directions: (Use a 3-5 Quart Slow Cooker)

Place all of the ingredients into your slow cooker and give it a stir. Cook on LOW for 8-10 hours, or on HIGH for 4-5 hours.

Remove about 2 cups of the soup broth and SLOWLY whisk in the heavy cream. This is "tempering" the milk so that your soup doesn't curdle. Slowly whisk your tempered milk/soup mixture back into your soup.

Turn your slow cooker up to HIGH. Now, slowly whisk in the corn starch, little by little. Keep whisking until it is well mixed. Let your soup cook about 15 minutes longer, whisking every few minutes. When the soup is thick enough to your liking, serve and enjoy!

Vegetarian Lasagna

L ASAGNA IS ONE OF MY favorite things to make in the slow cooker. I love that there is nothing to bubble over in my oven, hence, no awful mess to clean up! I've made lasagna with meat in it and without. Both are delicious! We don't like to eat meat every day, so this is one of the recipes we call on when we're not in the mood for meat.

I always use a slow cooker liner when I make lasagna in my slow cooker, however, because I strongly detest cleaning a crock with caked-on stuff! Whether you choose to use a disposable liner or not, be sure to spray your crock with non-stick spray.

If you're gluten-free, fear not, you can still make this! You will need to use gluten-free lasagna noodles. Because gluten-free noodles do not absorb liquid at the same rate as regular noodles, I'm listing the recipe below two ways, one gluten-free and one regular.

Servings: 6-10

Non-GF Ingredients:
- ½ - ¾ box of lasagna noodles
- 1 cup chopped zucchini
- 1 cup chopped yellow squash
- 1 10oz. package frozen chopped spinach, thawed, drained
- 1 cup cottage cheese
- 2-3 cups shredded mozzarella cheese
- 2 jars pasta sauce, or one batch of my Basic Pasta Sauce on page 16

Gluten-Free Ingredients:
- 1 box of brown rice lasagna noodles
- 1 cup chopped zucchini
- 1 cup chopped yellow squash
- 2 cups spinach leaves
- 1 cup cottage cheese
- 2-3 cups shredded mozzarella cheese
- 2 jars pasta sauce, or one batch of my Basic Pasta Sauce on page 16

Non-GF Directions: (Use a 6 Quart or larger Slow Cooker)

Spray your crock with non-stick spray. Now, ladle about ½ cup of your pasta sauce onto the bottom of your crock. Cover the bottom of the insert with lasagna noodles. It doesn't have to look pretty, but you want to cover the whole bottom.

Add a layer of half of your cottage cheese, half of your spinach, half your zucchini, half your yellow squash and 1/3 of your mozzarella cheese. Finish this layer with about 1/3 of your remaining pasta sauce.

Add another layer of lasagna noodles, the remaining cottage cheese, remaining spinach, remaining zucchini, remaining yellow squash, 1/3 of your mozzarella cheese and ½ of the remaining pasta sauce.

Add one last layer of lasagna noodles and spread the remaining sauce over the top.

Cook on HIGH for 2 hours, or on LOW for 3-4 hours.

About ½ hour before serving, sprinkle the top with the remaining mozzarella cheese and leave the lid off to help thicken up your lasagna. Turn your slow cooker off and let it sit for at least 20-30 minutes before serving.

Gluten-Free Directions: (Use a 6 Quart or larger Slow Cooker)

Spray your crock with non-stick spray. Now, ladle about ½ cup of your pasta sauce on the bottom of your crock. Cover the bottom of the insert with lasagna noodles. It doesn't have to look pretty, but you want to cover the whole bottom.

Add a layer of half of your cottage cheese, half of your spinach, half your zucchini, half your yellow squash and 1/3 of your mozzarella cheese. Finish this layer with about 1/3 of your remaining pasta sauce.

Add another layer of lasagna noodles, the remaining cottage cheese, remaining spinach, remaining zucchini, remaining yellow squash, 1/3 of your mozzarella cheese and ½ of the remaining pasta sauce.

Add one last layer of lasagna noodles and spread the remaining sauce over the top.

Cook on LOW for 5-6 hours, or on HIGH for 2.5-3 hours.

About ½ hour before serving, sprinkle the top with the remaining mozzarella cheese and leave the lid off to help thicken up your lasagna. Turn your slow cooker off and let it sit for at least 30 minutes before serving.

Index

C

About the Author

Hope Comerford is a BUSY mom, wife and full-time music teacher who makes no muss, no fuss recipes and posts them on her popular blog, "A Busy Mom's Slow Cooker Adventures." When not writing cookbooks, you can find her playing with her children, snuggling with her husband, singing, performing on stage, sewing, doing nails, or eating gluten-free cupcakes! You can find out more about her, and more of her recipes at www.slowcookeradventures.com. Connect with her on

Facebook – www.fb.com/SlowCookerAdventures

Twitter - @BusyCrockPotMom

Pinterest – pinterest.com/BusyCrockPotMom

My YouTube Channel – www.youtube.com/slowcookeradventures

23609711R00065

Made in the USA
Lexington, KY
19 June 2013